Rev.

Preston Memories

The publishers would like to thank the following companies for their

support in the production of this book

Cassidy + Ashton

Kirkham Grammar School

Myerscough College

Thompson Builders Merchants (Preston) Limited

R Walker & Sons (Preston) Limited

J Wareing & Son (Wrea Green) Limited

Bernard Watson

First published in Great Britain by True North Books Limited
England HX5 9AE
01422 377977

ISBN 1 903204 41 0

Text, design and origination by True North Books Limited
Printed and bound by The Amadeus Press Limited

Preston Memories

Contents

Introduction

'Preston is a fine town ... but not like Liverpool or Manchester,' was the verdict of the well-known novelist Daniel Defoe. Defoe visited the town in 1725, and although Preston has changed considerably since then, Proud Prestonians are still likely to express complete agreement with him - on both points!

In Defoe's time, Preston was essentially a market town, with three market days a week - Wednesdays, Fridays and Saturdays. Occupations in the area included agriculture and weaving, but it seems to have been the professional classes who were responsible for creating much of the town's wealth. From medieval times the law courts at Preston were used for various Borough and County sessions and sittings, and certainly an extraordinary number of lawyers were practising in the borough during the 18th and early 19th centuries. In 1825 Edward Baines published a complete trade directory which showed how many different trades and professions there were in Preston. There are, not surprisingly, more innkeepers than any other business; grocers form the second largest group, and attorneys the third largest, with the vast majority of the population being employed in the mills.

Although we normally associate the growth and prosperity of Preston with the Victorian period, the town was managing very nicely even before this and had long been a fashionable resort with it's own social season. From the mid-1700s onwards there was enough money around to erect some very substantial buildings, both public and private; a guild hall had been built by the Guild of 1762, and a number of gentlemen had residences in the town, though little evidence of these buildings has survived. It is also recorded that Preston was the first provincial town to lay on a gas supply, with the Preston Gas Lighting Company set up around 1815. All in all, Preston had a reputation as a very genteel place.

By 1825 a number of cotton mills were operating in Preston. Things had moved on a lot in the hundred years

Alderman H E Rhodes, Mayor of Preston, officially opens the new premises of the Preston Local Information Service and the Citizens Advice Bureau in 1946.

since Defoe visited the town, and the effects of the industrial revolution had begun to make themselves felt. Preston's first cotton-spinning factory had been set up in 1777 by two gentlemen by the names of Collison and Watson, and in 1791 a certain Mr John Horrocks arrived in Preston. Weaving remained a cottage industry for somewhat longer. When the Lancashire textile industry began to boom, Preston reaped the benefits along with the other textile towns. The concentration of industrial buildings in the town increased as more mills and factories were built, the population increased as people came to work in those mills and factories, and the town began to spread out as more houses were built to accommodate those people. In 1832 there were 310,000 spindles at work in the town, a decade later this had increased to 500,000 in 42 mills run by 10,500 hands. A number of buildings from this era are still there, although one which should be - the town hall designed by Sir Gilbert Scott, started in 1862 and completed in 1867 - has sadly been lost.

Textile manufacture was not the only industry that thrived in Preston during the Victorian era. Iron foundries were set up and engineering began in the town in 1867 with the North of England Carriage and Iron Co; there was a ready-made local market for mill machinery, but other items which were manufactured included printing presses and railway rolling stock, produced at the Strand Road engineering works from 1897. The arrival of the East Lancashire Railway was tremendously significant, both from a social and from an industrial point of view; the opening of Preston Dock towards the end of the 19th century, however, was not the runaway success that people might have hoped.

One very important strand running through Preston's history is, of course, the Guild tradition. In order for a medieval craftsman to carry on his business within the town, it was necessary for his name to be entered on the Guild roll. A fee was payable, in return for which he received certain rights and privileges. Proud Preston had a somewhat ambivalent attitude to incomers in those times. It became self-governing

Crowds gather in Market Place to await the arrival of King George VI and Queen Elizabeth upon the occasion of their visit to Preston in July 1938.

by Royal Charter in 1179; this basically freed its people from having to pay individual taxes to the lord of the manor, and instead the town paid an annual sum to the king each year. The town prospered under this system, but as a potential medieval tax haven it had to take steps to prevent people from the surrounding towns from moving in en masse. Various regulations were made, some more obviously useful than others. At one stage there was a law that prevented lodgings being let to outsiders without express permission from the authorities; and strangers were not allowed to buy anything at the market until an hour after it was opened to the townsfolk. Craftsmen and tradesmen who wanted to come and live in Preston had to apply to be admitted to the Guild, and there were strict Guild Orders which covered all aspects of trade in the town. At intervals it was necessary to hold a Guild Merchant to update the register of Guild members and to pass any new Orders that were needed. Once the business had been dealt with, celebrations were held; and this excellent tradition has been preserved. From

1542 the Guild celebrations have been held every 20 years, apart from a 30 year gap between 1922 and 1952 due to World War II. Readers will no doubt have their own recollections of the Preston Guilds that have taken place during their lifetimes, and will enjoy looking at the photographs of parades and festivities which are reproduced in this book. Other pictures in these pages reflect some of the changes that came about in the 20th century as our town adapted, in large ways and small, to accommodate modern lifestyles. We take another look at some of our old cinemas and theatres that were made redundant by television; some of the old housing that was demolished and replaced by new; some of the old streets that have been modernised in line with new shopping trends, or replaced by road layouts designed to cope with today's heavy traffic ... This collection of photographs is sure to bring back memories for readers who remember the town as it was, while those too young to remember will gain an insight into the Preston which their parents and grandparents used to know.

Street scenes

Some passers-by are glancing at the ruins, but as time passed they became an accepted feature of the townscape. Incredibly, the fire-gutted shell of the Town Hall stood there for 15 years. There were campaigns to have it rebuilt, but instead it was tidied up and made temporarily habitable, then demolished in 1962. The fire which reduced it to this state happened in the early hours of a freezing cold day in March 1947. Reports tell of how the Town Hall bells tolled as the clock tower collapsed, sounding the death knell of the famous building designed for the town by Sir Gilbert Scott. Its foundation stone was laid during Guild Week, 1862. It was built on the site of the old Town Hall, so that the elegant frontage, with the clock tower and this fine arcade of polished red granite pillars, faced Fishergate. Unfortunately this did not give a clear view of the front, which is why photographs of the Town Hall tend to show it from an angle, as in this case, rather than full face. The building cost over £70,000 - a lot of money in 1862 - and it replaced another town hall which stood there from 1782 to 1862 and cost £700 to build. It was hoped that Sir Gilbert Scott's fine Gothic creation would serve the town for centuries, as indeed it would have, barring disasters.

The writing on the wall leaves us in no doubt about the impending fate of the Hoop and Crown and its neighbour. The premises are coming down; Samuel's Gowns are getting rid of their winter stock at bargain prices, and one of Preston's very old-established inns has already called time for the last time and closed its doors for good. Rigby's, to the left of the gown shop, stayed put for many years, as did Travis' tobacconists, sandwiched between the Hoop and Crown and the Royal Hippodrome. The timing of the redevelopment made it easy to choose a name for the block which went up when these premises were pulled down: Coronation Chambers, named to commemorate the coronation of King George VI in 1937. A dancing school moved into the new building and remained there for some while, first as the Worsley School of Dancing and later as the Halford School of Dancing. Few of our readers will remember drinking at the Hoop and Crown, but the mention of the dancing school which took its place may well stir a memory or two of weekly dance lessons and the partners we danced with ...

Above: No prizes for working out who is about to set up shop on this corner! By the time World War II broke out, a new and grand Co-op store was standing here. Preston Co-op used to be much more than just a place to shop. One of the fundamental aims of the Co-operative Society was to help local families, particularly the less well-off. The Co-op put on excursions and organised concerts for the children, and it also ran classes in subjects such as household economy, needlework and nursing. The Co-operative movement

gathered momentum during the second half of the 19th century. A number of small co-operative societies were started in various parts of Preston, and in 1873 these amalgamated to form the Preston Industrial Co-operative Society. In the 1890s the Society opened its first big town-centre store in Ormskirk Road. This was officially called the Central Stores, but became better known as Fashion Corner. The Lancaster Road premises shown here were then built as an extension to Fashion Corner, and for a time the Co-op was THE place to go for good, reasonably-priced suits, hats, drapery and furniture of all kinds. But in the 1960s onwards the Co-op began to lose its customers to new, more aggressive high-street competitors, and in due course both its big stores became offices for central or local government departments.

Top: The covered market in Earl Street, which occupies the former Orchard (formerly an open meeting place) is quiet enough on this picture, but anyone who has ever shopped there will know what a lively, bustling and good-humoured atmosphere there is when the market is in full swing. Preston's heritage as a market town goes back many centuries, and the facilities provided for traders improved steadily as time went by. The impressive and ornate roof structure seen here was constructed during the 1870s, and initially posed something of an engineering challenge. The first attempt to put a roof up resulted in a pile of rubble when a section came crashing down, but the project was finally brought to a successful conclusion by local shipbuilders Joseph Allsup. This decorative feat of civil engineering has stood here since 1875, providing stallholders with welcome protection from the worst of the weather. Historically, Preston's market has done quite a bit of shuffling around between its various sites in the town. The covered stalls which used to stand in Market Place outside the Harris were moved in the 1970s, and it is a long time since dairy produce was sold outside the Corn Exchange at the Butter Market, although the site is still host to the annual pot fair in August.

The military-looking truck parked outside Lloyds Bank in Fishergate, once a very fine town house, is a portent of things to come. During the 1960s, not long after this picture was taken, the bank premises became an Army Careers Information Office. Up until 1960, the Army had not needed to go out of its way to attract young men into its ranks; National Service had continued to ensure a constant flow of new recruits. Between the end of the second world war and the end of conscription, no fewer than two and a quarter million men were called up. Some of them would have joined up anyway, but many young men dreaded their call-up, went unwillingly, and counted the days until their discharge.

But the only way to avoid military service was to be classed medically unfit, although in some cases it was possible to postpone for professional or academic reasons. The very last group of National Servicemen were required to join their regiments on 17 November 1960. Once the final batch of call-up papers had gone out, the ones who had escaped heaved a sigh of relief. From the Army's point of view, however, the end of National Service meant that from now on it had to find ways of persuading lads to join up voluntarily. So offices were opened in high streets, promoting the Armed Forces as an opportunity to learn a skilled trade, see the world and enjoy a fulfilling career.

The angle from which this photograph was taken emphasises the full height of Preston's fine war memorial, which stands around 70 foot up from its plinth. In order to erect this memorial here, the smaller South African War Memorial which previously occupied the spot was transferred to Avenham Park. The new memorial was designed by Sir Giles Gilbert Scott, famous as the architect of Liverpool Cathedral and also as the grandson of the renowned Sir Gilbert Scott. Sir Gilbert was responsible for the design of Preston's elegant Gothic town hall, built between 1862 and 1867, and destroyed by fire in 1947. The Admiral of the Fleet Earl Jellicoe of Scapa performed the official unveiling of Preston's new monument on 13th June, 1926. All over the country similar monuments were going up in solemn remembrance of those who gave up their lives during the first world war. The cost of victory had been high, but people consoled themselves by clinging to the belief that something had been achieved - that this really had been the war to end all wars. Few suspected that World War II was only just around the corner, and another generation of young men would be asked to put their lives on the line.

Preston's Corn Exchange has changed shape a number of times during its long and varied existence. It is recorded that the market here opened on 26 August 1824, though the inscription on its facade tells us it was built in MDCCCXXII (1822), and enlarged and restored in MDCCCLXXXII (1882). The building was described by Edward Baines in 1825 as 'a plain but handsome structure of brick, three stories high, of an oblong form ... ornamented with a stone pediment and cornice'. Records indicate that it served as corn exchange, meat market and cloth market, and contained small shops, but as time passed it was used less and less for trade. Following extensions it was no longer oblong, and canopies were added as seen on this photo-graph. It became primarily a venue for meetings and enter-tainments - the great Reform Bill meeting was held here in 1832 - although markets were still held outside it. An organ was installed - we note that a poster outside is advertising an organ recital - and the big bands of the 40s and 50s used to play there. Its canopies were removed around the time of the second world war, possibly for scrap. The demoli-tion of the main body of the building was fiercely opposed, and it was not removed until the early 1990s. The building began life in the 21st century as a pub known as the Flax and Firkin and has become part of the nightlife of modern Preston.

Below: Harrison's Hill, where this photograph was taken, used to be a street of terraced houses, as did Crown Street which runs off Harrison's Hill to the right, and Cragg's Row which can be seen in the background. This whole area, off Moor Lane, was cleared following a Demolition Order in 1958, and high-rise flats were built in place of the rows of terraces. Discussion has continued ever since - indeed, it started before the flats were completed - over whether this was a good idea or not. The benefits of doing this are obvious, the chief one being that one tower block can accommodate a whole streetful of people. The inherent drawbacks are equally plain, especially to the people who live there. A sound case can be made for each side of the argument, but at the end of the day the introduction of high-rise living to Preston accelerated the rehousing programme, and the experiment has certainly worked far better here and been more popular with the residents than in some other towns and cities, where similar schemes have resulted in wastelands which nobody wants to live in. Certainly tower blocks next to a windmill make for an interesting and possibly unique townscape; the Cragg's Row windmill was built around the 1760s, and was the site of the town's first 'cotton mill'. It was one of a number of windmills in the agricultural Preston of the 18th century.

Above: You can't have a collection of photographs of bygone Preston without showing a Ribble bus; so here one is, parked in front of the Harris Museum & Art Gallery. The first Ribble buses ran in Preston in 1919, and by 1924 the fleet had grown to more than 50 vehicles. The old Ribble Bus Station was replaced by a far bigger one when Tithebarn Street was reshaped by civic redevelopments in 1971. Buses were often to be seen lined up along this side of Market Place - just one of the many useful purposes which the square has served over the years. One way or another it has always been a focal point in the town. Before the Corn Exchange was built, this was Preston's main market place. A market, you might think, has always been a place where everybody can buy whatever they fancy, as long as they have the money; but, until the late 18th century, there used to be a regulation in force in Preston which prevented anybody who was not resident in the borough from making a purchase before ten o'clock in the morning, presumably so that the locals had the chance to snap up the best bargains first. Imagine trying to enforce that in this day and age!

Above: The young lady, who is stepping briskly away from the camera along Wards End, has a very 60s air about her - seamless stockings or, more likely, tights, and skirt rising above the knee. Sixties fashions became more extreme as the decade progressed. The older generation looked on in horror as their sons wore flowery shirts and grew their hair down past their collar, and their daughters wore shorter and shorter skirts, sometimes - horror of horrors - teamed up with knee-high 'wet-look' boots. New man-made fibres made these fashions possible; nylon tights allowed hemlines to rise without exposing stocking tops and suspenders, and the 'wet-look' was possible courtesy of the invention of stretch vinyl. The 60s was also the era of the Beatles, flower power - and Watneys Red Barrel. In the mid-20th century the brewing industry became a battlefield for the giants, and small breweries found it difficult to compete. Our young lady, who is probably going to the bus station, will pass the neon Thwaites Ales sign, and Thwaites, founded by Daniel Thwaite in 1807, is one of the Lancashire breweries which did survive. By the end of the 60s real ale devotees had become so worried about the disappearance of the small independents that CAMRA, the Campaign for Real Ale, was launched in 1972, to rekindle interest and appreciation of beers brewed using the traditional methods.

Looking down Fishergate into Church Street in the early 1960s, prominent names which can be picked out along the right hand side include the signs for the Gaumont cinema and Merigolds Garage. The Gaumont was doing all it could to attract audiences around this time. It is recorded that in 1959 the cinema invested £30,000 in a facelift and new facilities which included a state-of-the-art 50 foot curved screen. Its efforts to stay in business were not altogether wasted, as this establishment did manage to survive for longer than all Preston's other town centre cinemas. By the mid-60s it had become part of the Odeon chain, and as the Odeon it managed to keep going until 1991. It was quite an achievement to have kept up with so many technological advances from the early silent black-and-white films, which it started showing in 1928 as the New Victoria, right through to widescreen technicolor productions. Merigold's Garage also witnessed major changes within the British motor industry during the middle years of the 20th century, but many of the models which were around at that time are now regarded as classics - from the new Humber Snipe Imperial, available from Merigolds for £495 shortly before the outbreak of war, to the BMC Mini, launched in 1959 with a price tag of £496.

Originally named after the 13th century Franciscan Friary to which it led, Friargate has seen a great many changes over the years. The section seen in the foreground of our picture is of course now paved over and pedestrianised, with St George's shopping centre situated behind the photographer; it is hard to think of a street as being medieval when it has a modern shopping arcade next to it, but it is. The Harris building facing the camera is generally considered to be one of the finest buildings in Preston, and its fame has spread far and wide - both because of its own architectural merit, and because of the fascinating collections and exhibitions which it houses. Like a number of other important buildings in the town, its construction was planned so that a significant stage in its progress, either the laying of the foundation stone or the official opening of the premises, could be staged as part of a programme of Guild events. Readers may remember that the new Guild Hall was timetabled to be completed for the 1972 Guild, but delays caused by industrial disputes prevented this from working out. The Harris building, bequeathed by the Rev Edmund Harris, was completed by 1893, and generations of Prestonians have benefited from its presence ever since. It is now home to the town's central library.

The residents of Nile Street probably got quite used to saying cheese for the camera in the 1950s. After years of quietly minding its own affairs, putting up with the non-too-salubrious living conditions and getting on with the business of living, Nile Street suddenly found itself very much in the spotlight. Along with Bow Lane, Carlisle Street, Dover Street and Markland Street, it was named as part of the second big wave of compulsory purchase and demolition. The council had made a start on clearing some of the town's old pre-1850 housing after the first world war, but there was still a long way to go: just after the end of the second world war the town planners

had calculated that around 5,000 people in Preston were still living in overcrowded conditions and needed rehousing. The people behind this statistic probably had mixed feelings about it all. The houses along Nile Street show every sign of being well cared for. People have set up businesses here; there is a pub; clearly this is a little community which will cease to exist when the bulldozers move in. But the post-war policy was to knock down and replace rather than to renovate, and in total some 10,000 new council dwellings, comprising maisonettes, bungalows, ordinary houses and blocks of flats of various heights, were provided between 1921 and 1968.

A working dock, mill chimneys all over the place and not a tower block in sight; we have here an aerial view of a Preston whose economy is still rooted firmly in manufacturing and transport. Arguably the dock's main contribution to the fortunes of the town was in providing employment, as it almost invariably ran at a loss. All kinds of goods were brought ashore here, from bananas to Fiat cars, and in 1948 a roll-on roll-off lorry service to Larne was started. This grew into a major venture, with seven vessels being operated by the mid-50s - yet still the dock did not pay its way. In the end it had to be closed, and since then the extensive docklands area has found a multitude of new uses. Moving up from the dock basin, Shelley Mills can be seen. Cotton manufacture was responsible for Preston's growth during the Victorian era; not only were there literally dozens of mills, which employed mainly women, but there were also factories engaged in the production of mill machinery. The textile industry went into decline after the first world war. To the right of the dock can be seen the English Electric Works on West Strand, more commonly known as Strand Road, with the distinctive corrugated roofs; the English Electric company manufactured tramcars, fighter planes, rolling stock and much more besides, and was a major employer in the town.

Above: If you wanted to get from the old Ribble Bus Station in Tithebarn Street to Lancaster Road, the quickest way was to nip along Ward's End - but that meant going through the narrow passageway shown here with the rear of the Harris building on the left. The kiosk on the right always did a roaring trade on this busy thoroughfare. It was quite a dangerous area after dark, however, street crime did not prey overmuch on people's minds when this photograph was taken, probably in the mid-60s. In 1965, according to a Chambers dictionary of that year, 'to mug' simply meant 'to study hard', so apparently the crime of 'mugging' had not been invented. Certainly we used to be more trusting. We could leave bicycles propped up at the roadside and find them there when we came back, and we wandered around busy shops carrying open-topped shopping baskets, as often as not with our purses lying on top. Children could safely play out in the streets unsupervised. And the risk of being mugged might not be the only problem which this picture raises in the modern mind. TWO cigarette adverts? With no government health warnings? Even though George VI, who smoked heavily, had died of lung cancer in 1952, and scientists had produced evidence to show a connection between smoking and cancer, it all seemed rather far-fetched to most of us in 1965.

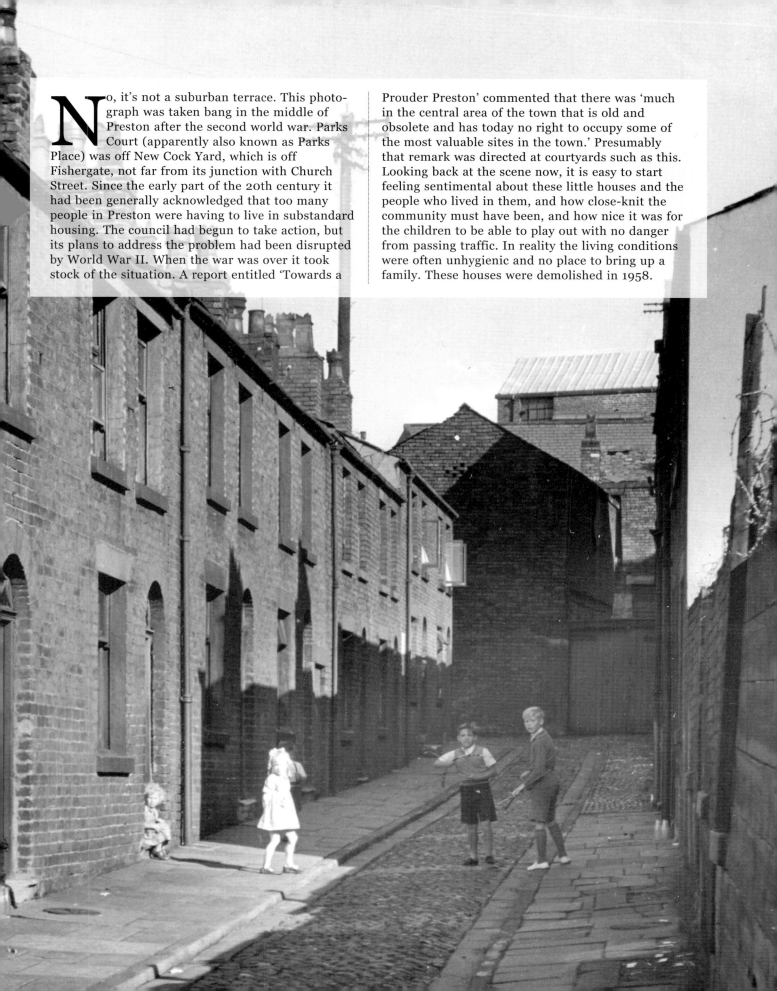

No, it's not a suburban terrace. This photograph was taken bang in the middle of Preston after the second world war. Parks Court (apparently also known as Parks Place) was off New Cock Yard, which is off Fishergate, not far from its junction with Church Street. Since the early part of the 20th century it had been generally acknowledged that too many people in Preston were having to live in substandard housing. The council had begun to take action, but its plans to address the problem had been disrupted by World War II. When the war was over it took stock of the situation. A report entitled 'Towards a Prouder Preston' commented that there was 'much in the central area of the town that is old and obsolete and has today no right to occupy some of the most valuable sites in the town.' Presumably that remark was directed at courtyards such as this. Looking back at the scene now, it is easy to start feeling sentimental about these little houses and the people who lived in them, and how close-knit the community must have been, and how nice it was for the children to be able to play out with no danger from passing traffic. In reality the living conditions were often unhygienic and no place to bring up a family. These houses were demolished in 1958.

Watson & Wrigley and the Co-op faced each other on this corner for many years. Watson & Wrigley, who had branches in other Lancashire towns, sold men's workwear and underwear. In 1938 - roughly the same era as our photograph, which is undated - Watson & Wrigley were offering bib-and-brace overalls for 3/6 (18p), and collars at three for a shilling (5p) in their annual winter sale. Men's collars used to be buttoned onto the shirt, and a new shirt normally came with at least two collars. They could be laundered separately, and if all your collars became frayed and the shirt itself was still good, you just bought another collar. When all-in-one shirts came onto the market, thrifty housewives disapproved because it seemed so wasteful to throw away a perfectly good shirt just because the collar was worn. Shirts bought from Watson & Wrigley before World War II were expected to last for years and years; they would be darned and patched, and as a last resort cut down into clothes for the kiddies. When they really could not be worn any longer, they would end up in the rag bag, an essential part of every housewife's toolkit, and the material would be used to patch other garments or to make fancy-dress outfits for the youngsters.

Above: Anybody who was not familiar with the Market Place area of Preston before the Market Hall was built may find this view difficult to identify. However, the tall building to the right should help: this is the rear of the former Co-op building on the corner of Lancaster Road. Up until the mid-60s, Liverpool Street used to be where the wholesale fruit, vegetable and flower traders had their warehouses, and if you walked through this part of the town first thing in the morning, the air smelled wonderful - the perfume of flowers mingled with the earthy smell of potatoes and root vegetables and the sharper scent of fresh fruit. After the end of World War II, Preston Dock became one of the UK's major points of entry for bananas and citrus fruit, so the standard of produce available from the local greengrocers was very high. The concept of charging extra for 'organic' farm produce would probably have seemed quite bizarre to the merchants who were sorting out their stock when this photograph was taken; how, they would have asked, can any fruit and veg possibly be inorganic? By the time the wholesale market moved out to Bow Lane, supermarkets were already moving in on an increasing number of food sectors, and their influence was one of the factors which changed not only consumers' shopping habits, but also the supply chains which brought the goods onto the shelves.

When the Corporation Arms was demolished along with most of Wharf Street to make way for the new Ringway, a reminder of a fraught period in Preston's history disappeared with it. In the Chartist riots of 1842, there were violent clashes between the cotton workers and the officers of the law. It is recorded that a group of protesters was driven at bayonet point from Fishergate to here. The troops then opened fire. Four protesters were shot dead in front of the Corporation Arms, and musketballs left marks on the inn's frontage. The Chartists were on a crusade to extend the franchise and reform Parliament. To the left of the Corporation Arms is a large sign advertising a visit from a contemporary crusader. Billy Graham was born William Franklin Graham in 1918 and began his worldwide evangelical campaign in 1947. It has been claimed that he preached to more people than anybody else in history. He had a powerful, theatrical style of addressing his audiences, and at the end of a meeting he asked people to 'make a decision for Christ' and give their names to his support workers. Billy Graham voiced strong views on politics as well as religion, and was a supporter of US intervention in Vietnam, which as all ex-hippies will know was one of the big political issues of the 1960s.

Above: Modern Preston presents a very different face to rail passengers who emerge from the station and look towards the town centre. There is still a pub on Butler Street, down the far side of the station - travelling is thirsty work, and there is a time-honoured tradition that wherever you have a railway station, you have a pub to go with it. But the Railway pub, which is the white building going by the name of the Railway & Commercial Hotel in this photograph, is now hemmed in on both sides by the Fishergate Centre. The high roofline of the distinctive brick and glass shopping mall dominates the corner spot and continues to the right of the pub, where the Debenham's building rises up. Car enthusiasts will immediately spot the Beetle which is heading for the station on our photograph; these characterful little cars, with their rear air-cooled engines, were extremely popular in the 1960s and became highly collectable in later years. Beer lovers, on the other hand, will see the prominent Lion Ales sign and remember the days when this was a familiar logo around Preston.

The vehicles parked along Fleet Street suggest this picture was taken during the early 1960s, with a couple of scooters parked along Fleet Street and a learner driver in a Ford Anglia preparing to negotiate the corner into Lune Street. The buildings on the right hand side of Fleet Street, and those in Lune Street facing the camera, somehow managed to survive the second half of the 20th century virtually intact, whilst the layout of the town changed around them. The tantalisingly semi-legible lettering on Marsh's building, on the corner of Fox Street, became even less legible. The businesses changed, of course, but what was a coffee bar on this photograph, with a Coca Cola sign outside, went into the next millennium as a bistro - not so very different. An inscription just below the apex of this building informs us that it was constructed in 1888, just a few years after the renovation and extension of the Corn Exchange. When this picture was taken the Corn Exchange would have been known as the Public Hall, and its future would have been far from certain. It was in the way of the planned Ringway, and although it was a historic building it was unused and rather run-down. However, an excellent compromise was reached: part of it was knocked down and what was left was restored, giving the Corn Exchange a new lease of life.

Events & occasions

Preston's Market Place was the place to be whenever there was an event of local or national significance in the offing - and the 20th century, with four coronations and a couple of World War victories, furnished a good many causes for national celebration. Which makes it a little difficult to be absolutely certain what has drawn this particular crowd; possibly the coronation of George VI in 1937, but more likely his visit to Preston the following year. That summer, King George and Queen Elizabeth went on a tour of the country to meet their subjects, and spent four days in Lancashire. They came to Preston on Tuesday 8th July, and were greeted in Market Place with a rousing rendition of the national anthem from the band of the 4th Battalion of the Loyal (North Lancashire) Regiment. Following the ceremonial presentation of prominent local people to the Royal couple, everybody sang God Save The King (one wonders how many times they heard Arne's famous tune during their tour!). The royal visitors then went on to lunch at County Hall, and from there to Moor Park to inspect a contingent of the British Legion. Their route along Moor Park Avenue was flanked by 14,000 school children, waving 14,000 miniature Union Jacks provided by the education authority - what a fine sight that must have been!

Even without his trademark cigar, the figure who has drawn such a crowd to Market Place will be instantly recognisable to many readers. Winston Churchill's words carried tremendous weight during World War II. In 1938, when Chamberlain, believing that he had secured a workable agreement with Hitler, had announced to the waiting nation that it was to be peace and not war, Churchill had been one of the few who remained sceptical. 'We have passed an awful milestone in our history,' was his comment. Then, as the war progressed, Chamberlain rapidly lost the confidence of the nation whilst Churchill, the British Bulldog, gained their support. In May 1940 Chamberlain resigned and Churchill took over. His astute and decisive handling of the war, along with his tough speeches and his tenacious courage, did a great deal to buoy up British morale. When victory was declared, Winston Churchill was cheered by millions. His visit to Preston on 27th June 1945 was part of a four-day tour of the Midlands, the north and Scotland, and crowds turned out to see him everywhere he went. Yet in the general election the following month, Winston Churchill lost and Labour won a landslide victory. In 1951 Churchill was voted back into power, but the following year he suffered a severe stroke. He died in 1965 at the age of 90.

Above: 'Never in the field of human conflict was so much owed by so many to so few.' Winston Churchill's words have gone down in the history books. 'The few' to whom he referred were, of course, the new breed of RAF pilots whose courage during the fierce airborne battles, which began during the summer of 1940, probably changed the outcome of the war. Germany, whose Luftwaffe launched an all-out attack, intended to destroy British Fighter Command. Britain had demonstrated that she still ruled the waves, so in order to prepare the way for invasion the Germans wanted to take control of the skies. Had they done so, they probably would have been able to carry out a successful invasion. Our pilots rose to the challenge, however, and in spite of notoriously sketchy training they proved more than a match for the Luftwaffe. The German bombers caused a great deal of damage to property and loss of life, but ultimately Germany abandoned the strategy, and there was no invasion. In recognition of the heroism displayed by the RAF pilots, a Battle of Britain Week was instituted in September 1946. Towns and cities all over the country paid tribute to their winged heroes, and here we see the opening March-Past in Preston. The RAF ensign was flown, and a Vampire jet circled above the town.

The streets of Preston echoed to the sound of marching boots on 13th May, 1945, as some 6,000 of our brave men and women took part in the Victory Parade. A lot of women put on new uniforms during World War II, some military and some not. In civilian life they became postal workers, bus drivers and conductresses, or Land Army girls; the girls on our photograph have taken one of the military options and joined the Auxiliary Territorial Service, the women's section of the army. ATS personnel were called upon to perform a wide variety of duties and undergo special training when required, involving, for instance, learning the principles of engineering and mastering new skills very quickly. Strict military discipline and drilling was also required of them. It was not an easy option, but the ATS performed valuable work and these smart ladies have every reason to hold their heads high as they take the salute. Germany had surrendered unconditionally on 7th May, the date now commemorated as VE day - Victory in Europe. This was a rather muted celebration in Preston as many men were prisoners of the Japanese and their fate was unknown. In fact the official end of hostilities did not come until 14th August, now known as VJ Day, when Japan finally surrendered.

V is for Victory: Britain has won the war and these evacuees can go back home to London, Liverpool and Manchester taller than when they left and many speaking with a different accent. Immediately after the declaration of war in 1939 an evacuation programme started to get children away from areas likely to be targeted by enemy bombs. However, when no bombs materialised many evacuated families began to drift back home. The following year air raids began in earnest, and a second major evacuation exercise took place. Each little evacuee was allowed one medium-sized bag containing sandwiches, a change of clothes, its gas mask and its favourite toy. It was then despatched with a label firmly attached to its small person, and with a pre-addressed envelope to be posted back to its parents when it was settled, giving the address of the host family. It was a worrying time; but in the event most of the kiddies who came to spend the war in villages near Preston enjoyed their stay and thrived, out of harm's way. Now that it is all over, they have been re-labelled and are about to return home, waved off by the Mayor, local dignitaries and the families they'd lived with; but we'd like to bet that some of these little faces came back to Preston in future years to visit the friends they made while they were here.

Both pages: In 1939 Britain's Prime Minister Chamberlain had made his announcement to the waiting people of Britain that '...this country is at war with Germany.' The country rolled up its sleeves and prepared for the inevitable. This war would be different from other wars. This time planes had the ability to fly further and carry a heavier load, and air raids were fully expected. Air raid shelters were obviously going to be needed, and shelters were built on open places across towns and cities.

By the time war was declared an army of volunteers of both sexes had already been recruited to form an Air Raid Protection service. At first ARP personnel were unpaid volunteers but when war broke out in September 1939 they became paid staff. It was their job to patrol specified areas, making

sure that no chinks of light broke the blackout restrictions, checking the safety of local residents, being alert for gas attacks, air raids and unexploded bombs. The exceptional work done by Air Raid Wardens in dealing with incendiaries, giving first aid to the injured, helping to rescue victims from their bombed-out properties, clearing away rubble, and a thousand and one other tasks became legendary; during the second world war nearly as many private citizens were killed as troops - and many of them were the gallant ARP wardens. At the beginning of the war Sir Anthony Eden, Secretary of State for War, appealed in a radio broadcast for men between 17 and 65 to make up a new force, the Local Defence Volunteers, to guard vulnerable points from possible Nazi attack. Within a very short time the first men were putting their names down. At first the new force had to improvise; there were no weapons to spare and men had to rely on sticks, shotguns handed in by local people, and on sheer determination . Weapons and uniforms did not become available for several months.

In July the Local Defence Volunteers were renamed the Home Guard, and by the following year were a force to be reckoned with. Television programmes such as 'Dad's Army' have unfortunately associated the Home Guard with comedy, but in fact they performed much important work. The Guard posted sentries to watch for possible aircraft or parachute landings at likely spots such as disused aerodromes, golf courses on the outskirts of towns, local parks and racecourses. They manned anti-aircraft rocket guns, liaised with other units and with regular troops, set up communications and organised balloon barrages.

Other preparations were hastily made. Place names and other identifying marks were obliterated to confuse the enemy about exactly where they were. Notices went up everywhere giving good advice to citizens on a number of issues. 'Keep Mum - she's not so dumb' warned people to take care

what kind of information they passed on, as the person they were speaking to could be an enemy.

Older readers will remember how difficult it was to find certain items in the shops during the war; combs, soap, cosmetics, hairgrips, elastic, buttons, zips - all were virtually impossible to buy as factories that once produced these items had been turned over to war work. Stockings were in short supply, and resourceful women resorted to colouring their legs with gravy browning or with a mixture of sand and water. Beetroot juice was found to be a good substitute for lipstick.

Clothes rationing was introduced in 1941, and everyone had 66 coupons per year. Eleven coupons would buy a dress, and sixteen were needed for a coat. The number of coupons was later reduced to 40 per person. People were required to save material where they could - ladies' hemlines went up considerably, and skirts were not allowed to have lots of pleats. Some found clever ways around the regulations by using materials that were not rationed. Blackout material could be embroidered and made into blouses or skirts, and dyed sugar sacks were turned into curtains.

By the late 20th century we had come to take our Citizens' Advice Bureaux for granted. Where else would we go for free advice when we end up victims of some kind of sharp practice, or at odds with the system, our neighbours or even our relatives? But prior to the second world war, there was no such thing. Preston's first Citizens' Advice Bureau was set up as a wartime measure and opened in October 1939, and by August 1946 it had responded to some 30,000 queries. Advice given in those early days covered a number of areas which thankfully we no longer have to worry about - bread rationing, clothing coupons, utility furniture and post-war

credits. But it also dealt with problems which have remained very much with us, such as pensions, trading problems, houses, family allowances and matrimonial problems. To start with, the CAB occupied offices in Ormskirk Road which were kindly provided free of charge by Preston Co-operative Society, and the Bureau remained there until the summer of 1946. Then new premises at 48 Lancaster Road were established for the Preston Local Information Service and Citizens' Advice Bureau. Here we see the door being officially opened by the Mayor, Alderman H E Rhodes, accompanied by a party of civic dignitaries, some of whom are wearing very fine hats.

Below: Crowds of Preston people have come to watch the end of an era, as the town's high-class milliners and haberdashery store goes up in smoke. Gooby's stood on the corner of Church Street and Tithebarn Street, and when you shopped at Gooby's you were served by well-trained shop assistants wearing black dresses, who went to a great deal of trouble to make sure you went away with exactly what you had gone in for. Fire broke out in the premises in March 1965, and in spite of the fire brigade's best efforts, nothing could be done to save Gooby's. Although it would have seemed heretical to say so at the time, perhaps Gooby's dramatic end was not altogether a bad thing. Times were changing, and the consumer's taste was changing, as is clearly demonstrated a little further along Church Street where the Empire has now been turned over to bingo. Up to this point Gooby's, Pegram's and other well-known local businesses of the old school had stood up to the incoming tide of national retail chains which were moving into every high street in Britain, but competition was becoming sharper and eventually many once-familiar names disappeared. Sad as it was to lose one of the town's leading stores like this, it would have been even sadder to watch the business go into decline and perhaps see the premises standing empty, waiting for the developers to move in.

How many readers remember the 1952 Preston Guild? After a break of 30 years, Church Street again became a riot of coloured pennants and flags for Guild celebrations, with its lamp standards spiralled in two colours like maypoles. During the course of the festivities, many a gay parade wended its merry way along Church Street, which was part of the processional route. Here we see the Women's Class from the Parish Church putting its variously-sized best feet forward, watched by a tremendous crowd. As well as all the traditional processions, the programme of festivities on that occasion included a Veteran Car Rally, an amusement fair in Miller Park, the Industrial Exhibition at Moore

Park and numerous other exhibitions throughout Preston, as well as sports, schools events, dancing, and much more. As usual the grand finale was a torchlight procession through the streets, culminating in a firework display in Avenham Park, and at midnight the National Anthem was played by massed bands in Market Square. The Ritz cinema, seen on the right, showed a special film entitled 'Proud Preston'. The only shadow on the proceedings was the absence of cattle, sheep, pigs and goats at the Royal Lancashire Show, held at Ashton Park in Guild Week. There had been an outbreak of foot and mouth some 20 miles from Penrith, and agricultural shows were excluding cloven-hoofed animals, for fear of spreading the disease.

Above: Edward Baines, who wrote a comprehensive work on life in Lancashire in the early 19th century, was very impressed by the 'freedom from excess, and the elegance and refinement of the entertainments' of the Preston Guild - which he attributed to the fact that ladies take part in the celebrations. Certainly these ladies, with their pretty frocks and their highly artistic banner, will add a touch of feminine elegance to the parade. This tableau was photographed in Fulwood in 1952, and the photographer has created a clever visual effect with a banner showing the Wesleyan church fluttering in front of the real thing. The people of Preston had waited a long time to celebrate this particular Guild Merchant. For almost 400 years the pattern of holding the Guild celebrations at 20-year intervals had been followed. The first Guild Merchant is recorded

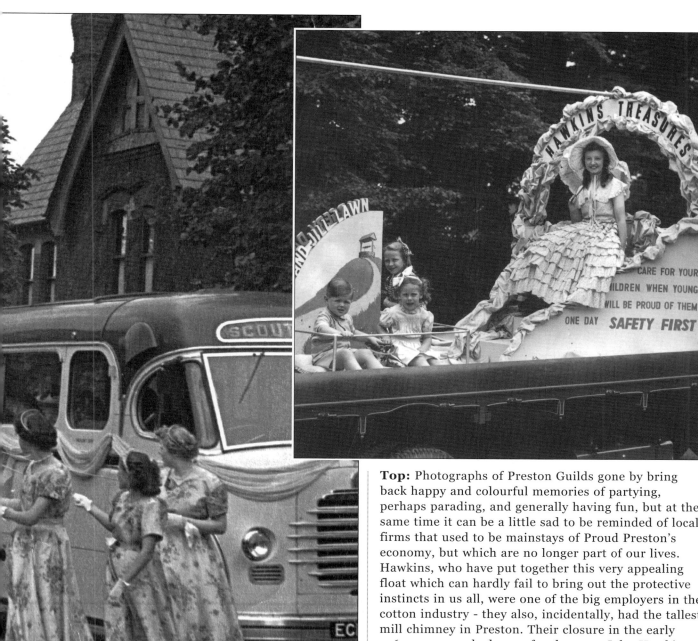

Top: Photographs of Preston Guilds gone by bring back happy and colourful memories of partying, perhaps parading, and generally having fun, but at the same time it can be a little sad to be reminded of local firms that used to be mainstays of Proud Preston's economy, but which are no longer part of our lives. Hawkins, who have put together this very appealing float which can hardly fail to bring out the protective instincts in us all, were one of the big employers in the cotton industry - they also, incidentally, had the tallest mill chimney in Preston. Their closure in the early 1960s was very bad news for the area. John Hawkins established his business at Greenbank Mills in 1836, and over the years the John Hawkins & Co empire grew and spread. The other big local millowners were Horrocks, Crewdson & Co who had various premises including the Yard Works on Stanley Street, Centenary Mills on New Hall Lane, and Fishwick Mills. Certainly the representatives of the cotton industry used to make a grand spectacle in the Guild parades. The origins of the Guild Merchant celebrations are, after all, firmly rooted in the local trades. The periodic updating of the names on the Guild registers ensured that tradesmen continued to enjoy the privileges to which they were entitled, and provided an opportunity for each of the guilds to display their achievements.

as having taken place in Saxon Times, and between then and 1542 the event was staged at irregular intervals. The 20-year cycle was then established, and held good up to and including the Guild of 1922. But with the second world war in progress, there was no possibility of organising celebrations in 1942. When peace was restored it was decided to set the next date at 1952, and the 20-year interval has been resumed from there.

At leisure

This photograph was taken before Foster's foundry in Lancaster Road was demolished and the site taken over by the NW Electricity Board, who built a showroom there. Nearer to the camera is the entrance to Wally's Dance Club, and careful examination of the photograph with a magnifying glass reveals that the words Adriatic School of Dancing are just visible on the door. Wally Hobkirk was a well-known dance instructor who between the 1940s and 1980s taught generations of local people to trip the light fantastic. There is an interesting story about the Adriatic ballroom: the floor was made out of timbers taken from the good ship Adriatic, a huge White Star liner that came to Preston in 1899 to be broken up by Thomas Ward's big shipbreaking company alongside the river Ribble. That was how the Adriatic ballroom got its name, and it is rather nice to think that the ship lived on in this way. Other popular Preston ballrooms included the Regent on Tithebarn Street, the Public Hall which was really the Corn Exchange, and the Queen's Hall, just round the corner from the Adriatic at Saul Street Baths. The baths, which used to be where the Crown Courts now are, had a small pool and a large pool, and during the winter the large pool was boarded over and used for dancing.

Below: Many of Preston's public buildings can trace their origins back to Guild years, and so it was with the original Theatre Royal, which was built on Fishergate to provide somewhere to stage theatrical performances during the 1802 Preston Guild. The original theatre looked nothing like this one, however; it was a very small, plain, squarish building. Towards the end of the 19th century it was rebuilt, and as we can see it was enlarged and given a nice facade. We can also see that by the middle of the 20th century it had fallen into a sad state of disrepair. In 1958 it was demolished, and work began on the new luxury cinema which was to take its place. The ABC opened on 14th March 1959 with a showing of the Reluctant Debutante, starring Rex Harrison and Kay Kendall, and with 1,400 seats was the biggest cinema in town. But the timing was unfortunate, as it was not long before television's impact on cinema audiences began to bite. In the early 70s the auditorium was reduced in size, and in September 1982 the ABC was closed. Oddly, out of all Preston's cinemas the ABC is the one that many people seem to remember best, and yet it showed films for only 23 years. The building itself stood there empty for another four years before being pulled down.

Y ou can't have a fortnight of festivities without lots and lots of dancing. This was certainly acknowledged to be the case in 1952, so the organisers of the Preston Guild earmarked £1,100 especially for marquee dances. A dance was held in Miller Park just about every night, in addition to a series of more formal balls at the Public Hall. The 1952 Preston Guild celebrations were allocated a total budget of over £41,000 (which was a lot of money then), of which £33,000 was to be funded out of the rates, with the rest being covered by income generated by the celebrations. Our photograph was taken at one of the

marquee dances in Miller Park, and judging from the stance of the dancers we think the band is playing a waltz. The days of disco were still more than a decade away, but as the 50s progressed rock and roll would arrive on the scene, bringing a new range of dance routines as an alternative to the time-honoured ballroom steps. Boys became Teds, with greased-back hair and quiffs, and they wore crepe-soled shoes, drainpipe trousers and long drape jackets cut in the Edwardian style from which they got the name of Teddy-boys. And Elvis Presley shocked the nation simply by gyrating his hips. How easily-shockable we were in those days!

Preston's grand, classically-styled Palladium was opened in 1915. In 1938 it was joined by the Ritz cinema, and the two establishments stood opposite each other in Church Street for many years, run by the same owners. Those were the days when a town needed numerous places of public entertainment; the concept of 'home entertainment' as we know it had not been invented. At home families played games, wound up the record player and listened to a few records, and generally made their own fun, but for an afternoon's or evening's entertainment, you got dressed up and went out - dancing, to the theatre or to the cinema. Television changed all that, and from the late 1950s onwards Preston's places of entertainment began falling like ninepins. The Palladium Picture House was demolished around 1970, while the Ritz, which had once been regarded as the most super cinema imaginable, was turned into a bingo hall. The Theatre Royal and the Royal Hippodrome bit the dust in 1959, and the Princes Theatre came down in 1964, as did the King's Palace. The Palace, as the latter was generally known, had been converted into a cinema from a vaudeville theatre, and in 1955 was actually one of the first cinemas to close. The Odeon held out longest of all the town centre cinemas, finally closing in 1991.

On the move

It is probably no exaggeration to say that the arrival of the railway in the mid 19th century opened up exciting new possibilities for everybody, from the rich and famous to the ordinary working man and his family. Queen Victoria travelled by train, and it is recorded that King George V even drove the GWR locomotive 'Windsor Castle' for a short distance when he visited Swindon in 1924. The novelist Charles Dickens used to travel through Preston station, and although he did not go into much detail in his letters about the station itself, he did make several very complimentary comments about 'the young lady who sells the papers'. Newspaper stands, like pubs, were quick to establish close relationships with railway stations, and W H Smith wasted no time in moving in. By the 1870s Smith's was already developing a large network of outlets at main line stations throughout the country. On this basis it could be claimed that W H Smith was in fact the nation's first chain store; the turn of the 20th century saw an increasing number of retail chains being built up, with names such as Maypole Dairy, Lipton and Boots amongst them - but W H Smith did it first.

Railway enthusiasts will know that trains for East Lancashire used to use a separate but connected area of Preston Station which was always referred to as the East Lancashire Platform. This portion of the station has now been completely demolished. The train now standing at the East Lancashire Platform is an ex-Midland 4-4-0. The date of our photograph is given as October 1956; the post-war years were a period of major reorganisation within the railways, following the nationalisation of Britain's rail network. As well as all the administrative restructuring, there was also the question of how the trains of the future

should be powered, and this became quite a talking-point amongst train-lovers, who became very knowledgeable on the relative advantages and disadvantages of steam, electricity and diesel. Preston, the home of English Electric, had a vested interest in this debate, and probably at the very time this photograph was taken the most

famous diesel electric locomotive ever built was under construction in the West Works. The Deltic, used on the London to Edinburgh service, had a power output of 3,300hp and was quite simply the most powerful single unit diesel electric locomotive known to man. A few of these marvellous engines have been preserved.

Above: The Morris Mini-Minor and the Austin Seven were launched simultaneously in 1959, with the only difference being the badge - so 'badge engineering' is not as new a phenomenon as we may think. Following the merger which produced BMC in the early 1950s, Morris Motors and Austin continued to produce looka-like models such as the Morris Oxford and Austin Cambridge, and the 1100/1300 ranges. The legendary Mini Cooper was launched in 1961, extending the Mini's market to those who demanded high performance as well as practical advantages. Economical, easy to manoeuvre and fun, Sir Alec Issigonis' brainchild and its descendants became pretty much ubiquitous during the 1960s. The other vehicle on our photograph is a Ford Thames van, similar to the Anglia saloon, and bears one of the early desig-nated Lancashire County registrations which included TB, TC, TD and TE. The location of the photograph may prove more tricky to identify, especially for younger readers. This bit of Preston was completely redeveloped around 1970, when it was earmarked as the site for a new Civic Hall. The Ward's End which in modern Preston runs off Lancaster Road between the Guild Hall and the Stanley Arms is completely different from the Ward's End which existed prior to the redevelopment.

What a novel way to spend a summer's afternoon in the 1950s: sitting in a traffic jam on London Road. We suspect something out of the ordinary must have happened to cause this tailback, though we have no way of knowing. Most people were just beginning to discover the joys of motoring around this time, and certainly they had many new experiences to look forward to. Motorways, for instance. The Preston by-pass, the first stretch of motorway in Britain, was opened in December 1958, and many motorists went for a drive along it just to see what it was like. It was subsequently absorbed by the M6. It must be hard for later generations to imagine how strange and exciting motorways seemed to us at first. There were new rules about lane discipline for us to learn - and sales of wing mirrors and door mirrors from car accessory shops must have rocketed; external mirrors were not generally factory-fitted as standard, as can be seen from this picture, but suddenly we needed them. The most difficult thing to learn, however, was how to get on and off the motorway; sliproads were something completely new. We never thought, then, that those miles and miles of tarmac would ever get congested like ordinary roads! And while we wait for the London Road jam to clear, classic car enthusiasts can have fun seeing how many models they can identify. There's a Rover, a split-screen Morris Minor ...

Sporting life

We believe that these lovely lasses are Dick, Kerr's original ladies' football team. They might look demure and well-behaved, with their cute little striped bonnets, their nice clean shirts and their neatly-laced boots - but don't you believe it; from the opening kick to the final whistle, they play to win! It all began during World War I when a group of women workers at Dick, Kerr's had the bright idea of playing football to raise money for the Moor Park Military Hospital. Dick, Kerr's tramworks started in East Works on Strand Road, and West Works were added at a later date; the West Works subsequently became the GEC factory. The ladies' football scheme succeeded not only as a fund-raising venture but also as a football team, and marked the beginning of a great tradition. Their fame spread far and wide, and this continued over the years with a succession of fine Dick, Kerr's ladies' teams showing just what the women of Preston could do, including being Champions of the World. Dick, Kerr's workers were fortunate in having good sports facilities: Ashton Park used to be the firm's sports ground, and was frequently used by Preston North End as a practice pitch.

Preston's footballers were certainly on a roll in 1938. Preston North End had won the Cup; and, not to be outdone, the Preston Ladies travelled to the St Anne's Road stadium in Blackburn during August holiday week to meet the Edinburgh Ladies. Our photograph shows the captains flipping the coin. Spectators seem rather thin on the ground, though the trip to Blackburn to watch the ladies would have been well worthwhile as by all accounts the Preston women delivered a very impressive performance. They won a 5-1 victory, with M Thornborough scoring three goals and Lily Parr, as good a player as Alec James, scoring two. Over the years Preston has produced some fine women footballers, and has had a long involvement in the North West Women's Football League. The ladies' teams from Dick, Kerr's works were quite a phenomenon during the first half of the century. Perhaps it is as well that women's football never caught the attention of the media in the way that men's football did. The women's game was able to retain its innocence as changes overtook the men's game: hooliganism, transfer fees soaring higher and higher, and good footballers being elevated to superstar status and subjected to all the pressures that this brings. One way and another, the outside influences from politicians, big business and the tabloids seem to have taken football a long way from its simple sporting roots.

People of both sexes and all ages have come to join in the excitement, crammed into Market Place or hanging out of the upstairs windows of Nottingham House, Barratts, Freeman Hardy Willis and no doubt other buildings too. This is a 1938-style football crowd - guaranteed hooligan-free, largely sober, and easily controlled by a handful of policemen and police horses with no riot gear. They are celebrating Preston North End's most glorious achievement of the 20th century. Captained by Tom Smith, the team hung on grimly against Huddersfield Town at the Wembley cup final, and finally netted the winning goal in extra time - and this is their well-earned moment of glory as they arrive home to a heroes' welcome in their Leyland Motors coach operated by Scout Motors. No doubt some in the crowd would remember North End's golden hour of the previous century. The legendary team of 1888-9, known as the Old Invincibles, set some amazing records. They won the League Championship without losing a single match (though it was easier in those days since there weren't as many clubs in the league); they won the English Cup without conceding a single goal. A number of Old Invincibles were still living in 1938, and a few were even able to travel to Wembley to see the match and, no doubt, re-live happy memories.

Below: Sir Tom Finney is seen here scoring one of the grand total of 210 goals which he netted for Preston North End in League and Cup games. During his career he also played for England in 76 matches. Tom was born in Deepdale in April 1922, and showed talent from an early age - though when Preston Schoolboys reached the final of the 1936 English Schools Trophy, Tom was included as reserve, as he was judged too small to be selected. He went on to enjoy a legendary career, during which he was voted Footballer of the Year twice. He stayed loyal to his home town, making his final appearance for Preston North End in April 1960 and becoming the club's President; he was also a This Is Your Life subject, received the Freedom of the Borough of Preston in 1979, and a CBE in 1992. The

match seen here was played against Blackburn Rovers on 3 October 1959 with Preston North End winning 4-1 in front of a crowd of 41,694, and it is interesting that both sides were among the original 12 clubs that formed the football league in 1888. The other ten were Aston Villa, Wolverhampton Wanderers, Bolton Wanderers, West Bromwich Albion, Accrington, Everton, Burnley, Stoke, Derby County and Nottingham County. Winners of the League and Cup double in the very first season, 1888-89, were - Preston North End!

Bottom: Goodness knows how the Hargreaves delivery down by Lipton's managed to get itself mixed up in this crowd - didn't the driver know that the Preston North End players were due to arrive in the Flag Market from Cheapside to show us the Cup? If not, he must have been the only person in Preston who didn't! North End met Huddersfield Town in the final at Wembley on Saturday, 30th April 1938, and that afternoon Preston was like a ghost town. Everybody was either down at Wembley, or at home with their ears glued to the wireless. It was the second year in succession that Preston had reached the final; the previous year they had lost 3-1 to Sunderland. This time North End didn't let any goals in, but neither, it seemed, could they manage to score. The match went into extra time, and the fans who had travelled to Wembley began to worry about catching the Football Special back home. With the final whistle approaching and still no score, many of them left for their train - and then, less than half a minute from the end of extra time, Mutch scored from a penalty. So the Cup came back to Preston, and on Monday evening the town turned out to pay tribute to their victorious team.

Shopping spree

We believe this photograph of Lune Street was taken in the late 1950s. The volume of traffic indicates that car ownership is on the up in Preston and town centre congestion is beginning to be a problem. National statistics show that in 1953, one adult in every twenty-four had a car. This rose dramatically in the next ten years, and by 1963 one adult in seven was a car owner. Prompted no doubt by scenes like this, Preston realised that its one-way traffic flows were not the answer, and more radical changes would need to be made to the road layout. Under the existing system, through traffic used to go right across the middle of the town. Fishergate, Church Street, Lune Street and the full length of Friargate were all main routes through Preston. Clearly cars needed to be able to get from one side of Preston to the other without going through the shopping streets and making life a misery for the pedestrians. To make this possible, a new road would have to be created. The notion of constructing a ring road was, in the 1950s, a controversial proposition; but by 1957 a route had already been sketched out. It was to be another ten years, however, before work on the Ringway actually started.

How nice it must have been, to stand and look in Pegram's window on Lune Street, in the late 1950s and not have to worry about ration coupons! People who were not born until after the war sometimes assume that as soon as the war ended, rationing ended as well, but this was far from the case; in fact it got worse after the war, with bread rationed for the first time in 1946. Sweets briefly came off ration in 1949, but in 1951 they went back on, and from then until 1954 each person was allowed six ounces of sweets a week. Food rationing stayed with us in some form or another for over 14 years in all. The first items to be rationed were bacon, ham, sugar and butter, and this came into effect on 8th January, 1940. As time went on the weekly food ration became tighter, and many imported foods, such as bananas, disappeared completely. It was not only food that was rationed, either; just about everything was, from soap to furniture. For instance, everybody had an annual clothing allowance and had to hand over coupons for each garment they purchased: 16 for a man's overcoat, 11 for a woman's dress, and so on. Goodness, it was complicated - and how wonderful it was when you could once again buy as much as you liked of whatever caught your eye.

Shops along Fishergate come and go, and sometimes, when times are prosperous, they expand or rebuild their premises. Owen & Owen's department store went, though the rather unusual building is still there with different occupants. British Home Stores built themselves a more modern brick-faced store at the end of the 1960s, from which they continued to serve Preston for the rest of the century and beyond. The exclusion of through traffic has made shopping in this street much more pleasant, and a general tidying up of Fishergate in the 1980s provided seating where shoppers can sit and survey the scene. A number of Victorian buildings have survived along the stretch which is visible farther away from the camera, rubbing shoulders with the contrasting structures that have sprung up between them and giving the street a varied and interesting character. Fishergate and Church Street have both existed for a very long time, in contrast with Lancaster Road which is much newer. One of Church Street's oldest buildings is the bank just round the corner from the junction with Lancaster Road, opposite the Old Bull public house. Having been a bank since 1816, it became vacant around the turn of the 21st century. At the time of writing it was standing empty, possibly contemplating a change of career as a wine bar.

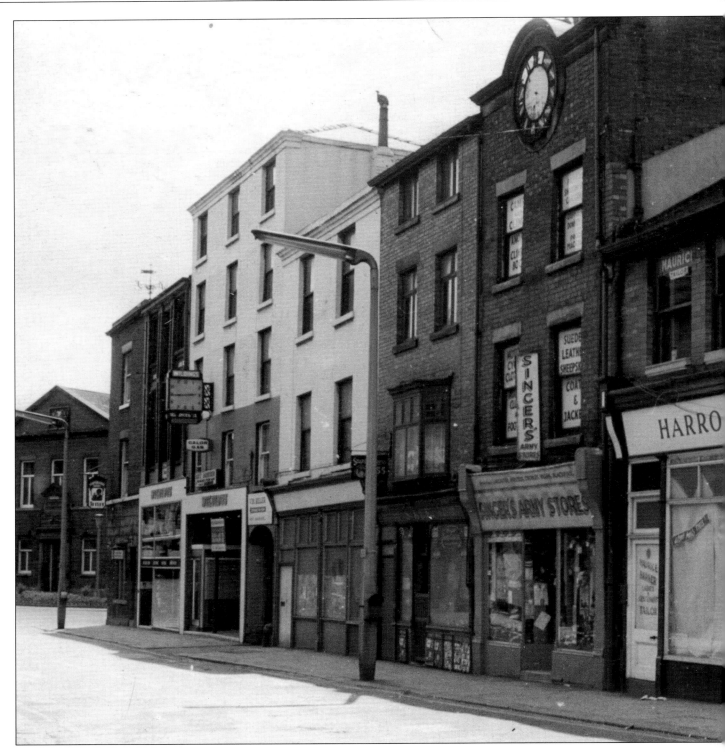

Above: The parade of shops shown here vanished without trace when the Ringway came into being. Some of the businesses relocated to other parts of Preston: the long-established Singer's Army Stores, for one, continued to serve Prestonians who enjoyed the outdoor life for the rest of the 20th century and beyond. The clock-face seen atop Singer's premises had had no hands for a long time; you could tell the time from Wilding's more modern clock a little further along the street, but clocks without hands generally tend to be a sign that an area which was once prosperous is going downhill. The building on the corner nearest the camera was already suffering from an identity crisis when this photograph was taken. Although the shop has been taken over by Harrops Fashion Centre, the name of its illustrious former proprietors was set in stone

Top: Pictured here is Lune Street, heading towards Friargate. Lune Street had to be pruned to clear the way for the Ringway, which was to transform the spot where Lune Street and Friargate used to merge. So this bit of Lune Street was demolished in 1967, and these are some of the assorted businesses which had to up sticks. Modern commercial premises are generally built either as units within a large retail complex, or as single storey buildings with a prominent shop window, a sales area, room for storage and a few basic facilities for the staff. In Victorian times, the distinction between residential and business properties was less clear cut. Business proprietors and their families generally lived above their businesses, and some large retailers provided live-in accommodation for their staff as well. So the buildings were substantial, with numerous rooms above them. In later years it became less common for people to live and work within the same four walls, partly because the retail chains were taking over from the small family business. With the upper floors no longer required for living accommodation, they could be let out to other businesses. The upper floors of Victorian shop premises often attract practitioners in the legal, insurance, accounting and other professions which do not need a large shop window, though in this picture we see that a couple of hairdressers have set up salon above Wildings celebrated light shop.

along the roofline on both its Lune Street and its Friargate frontage. Pegram's was a superior grocers and provisions merchant, and occupied this corner for many, many years. Looking along to the far end of the parade, readers accustomed to the modern layout in this part of town will find it very odd to see the Corn Exchange with buildings this side of it, rather than set back from Ringway in its own little courtyard.

Above: Two things of interest in this photograph are firstly, the very fine example of a Ford Classic which is parked on the left hand side of Fox Street as we look down towards Fleet Street, and secondly, the view of the Public Hall facing us at the bottom. The Public Hall, or Corn Exchange, used to stretch back much further than it does now, occupying virtually the full length of the north side of Fleet Street from Lune Street to what is now Corporation Street, though when the Corn Exchange was first built Corporation Street did not exist. At the far side of the Public Hall, where the Ringway now is, there used to be another street called Wharf Street, running parallel with Fleet Street. Much of Wharf Street disappeared in 1963 in preparation for the Ringway. These same preparations also involved demolishing a significant portion of the Public Hall. Over the years the Public Hall, with its gallery and spacious floor area, had been used for a wide variety of public meetings and entertainments, and during the 1952 Guild celebrations it made a splendid venue for the more formal balls; the town was at that point without a Guild Hall, as the old one had been in the old Town Hall which burnt down in 1947, and the new Guild Hall had yet to be built.

The further away from the camera you look, the fewer the changes. The buildings which can be seen to the far side of Marks & Spencer have by and large remained structurally unaltered, though there are new developments further along. Marks & Spencer's frontage remained similar, with the most striking difference being that the facade no longer has a pediment bearing the store's name. Manfield & Sons' shoe shop, with the entrance to Manfield Chambers next to it, has been replaced by a quite different building. Both shops were in Fishergate in the very early 1900s. When Mr Michael Marks and Mr Tom

Spencer took small premises to the left of Manfield and opened a Preston branch of their Bazaar chain, nobody realised that M & S was one day going be a household name and a British institution. By 1929 Messrs Marks and Spencer had acquired their new site, cleared it and built their own distinctive store, on the same pattern as the Marks & Spencer buildings which were going up in high streets all over the country at that time. Clearing the site meant demolishing the old Central Club building, which used to be used by the Preston Scientific Society. The new Marks & Sparks was opened in the summer of 1929, and later the store expanded again.

Although the 20th century was without a doubt a golden age for the motor car, the fortunes of Britain's various car manufacturers were very mixed. On the right of this photograph is a three-wheeler, preparing to emerge into Lune Street. These little cars offer many advantages, but somehow three-wheeled vehicles never really caught on. The Bond factory in Ribbleton made some superb little three-wheelers. The very first model to be manufactured there in 1950 had a 125cc two-stroke Villiers engine and gave up to 100 miles per gallon - better than the BMC Mini. Bond made three-wheeled and four-wheeled cars with fibreglass bodies; this meant that they were extremely light, which as well as giving excellent fuel consumption made them very nippy. Many models were available with roll-back canvas hoods - a little 'extra' that the BMC Mini did not normally offer. But the fact was that most motorists seemed to want metal cars with four wheels. In the late 1960s Bond had another stab at capturing the youth market, launching a bright orange Bond Bug which one motoring magazine compared to 'a demented wedge of Leicester cheese'. On the whole the critics liked the car, but it still failed to sell in sufficient numbers, and Bond remained one of the marques that never did get the recognition it deserved.

Outside Billsborough's shop on Lune Street are several large advertisements aimed at the DIY decorator. By the end of the 20th century it had become the norm for the majority of households to do some if not all of their decorating themselves. However, this trend did not begin until after the second world war. New developments in paints, glues and synthetic building materials around that time made products more user-friendly. Now unskilled workmen - or women - could do their own decorating and home improvements with perfectly adequate results, and more cheaply than if they had called in the professionals. The idea seemed so radical that when the major paint manufacturers came to market these new products, they were very wary of explicitly targeting the amateur decorator, as they feared that by doing so they would alienate their traditional client base of trade customers - and they were not even sure whether the public would buy. They need not have worried; Dulux, launched onto the retail market in 1953, soon became a household name, and the trade accepted that a new market had opened up. During the 1950s and 60s we turned into a nation of keen DIY-ers. Many young couples who married and set up home after the war discovered the delights of painting, papering and putting up shelves - and, if the walls were thin, annoying their new neighbours into the bargain. Sadly, many of these buildings were demolished in the early 1960s to make way for St George's shopping centre. The ginnel next to Billsborough's shop led to a large number of well-known ancient buildings including a celebrated pie shop.

Above: This building is still there, on the corner of Lancaster Road and Church Street opposite the Miller Arcade. Church Street has existed since medieval times, but Lancaster Road was not laid out until the Victorian era. At the same time Corporation Street was built on the other side of the town centre as a relief road for Lower Friargate. Did the proposals to construct these roads cause as much consternation amongst the Victorian Prestonians as the planned Ringway did during the 1960s, we wonder? During the last 50 years or so, rebuilding in the town centre has resulted in an eclectic mix of building styles; sometimes whole streets were cleared away and redeveloped, sometimes just one building was knocked down and replaced by a new one. Starkie's name, seen in this photograph, has been preserved in Starkie's Chambers, though the retail business has disappeared and few people nowadays ever refer to this corner as Starkie's Corner. The Leather Shop was established as long ago as 1917 and so had been operating for a very long time indeed when this photograph was taken, probably in the 1960s.

Narrow passageways and courtyards leading off main streets, sometimes through a gate or archway, are a typical feature of towns which began as medieval settlements. Preston still has a good number of these alleyways, but many have been cleared to make way for large retail complexes and - in the case of the area pictured here - the Guild Hall development. Ward's End used to be a little medieval passage that ran off Lancaster Road just to the left of the Ribble Office, and this little backstreet, which was called Cheetham Street, ran off Ward's End. By the early 1970s all the buildings in both streets had been flattened. Looking back over the second half of the 20th century, it does seem that a great deal of demolition happened in a few short decades. The main thrust in the 1950s was the clearance of what was deemed unfit housing and the provision of new accommodation, often in the form of high-rise flats. In the 1960s most of the chaos was at the west side of town where the Ringway was being built. A few years later it was all happening around Tithebarn Street, with a huge new bus station and the new Guild Hall going up. Then it was Fishergate's turn. Tower blocks, new roads, futuristic new architecture and fancy new shopping centres ... it was a lot to take in.

At work

A typical scene at Preston Dock in its heyday: timber and wood pulp were for a long time major imports, along with livestock, oil, potatoes and, later on, bananas and citrus fruit. Exports included coal, paper and machinery. Although Preston has had a port since early times, when ships would simply tie up along the river bank, it was not until the late 19th century that the Ribble was dredged to make it navigable by bigger ships, and a new dock was built. Preston Dock was opened by the Duke of Edinburgh in 1892. It had a water area of 40 acres, which made it the biggest single dock in the country at the time of its opening, and it was equipped to deal with different types of cargo, but nonetheless the dock consistently operated at a loss for the first half of the 20th century, saddled with the debt from its construction, and was subsidised through the Ribble Rate. During World War II the dock, known as the Albert Edward, played an invaluable role in handling large shipments of food supplies, raw materials and munitions. After the war the gross income of the Dock increased and during the 1950s and 1960s it brought an enormous amount of business to the town, but operating costs remained high, there was keen competition from other ports and it closed in 1981 and the area was redeveloped.

Above: It's shirt-sleeve weather, and there are a lot of sandbags to stack - make no mistake, preparing for war is hard work! Towns and cities all over Britain were taking measures to protect their public buildings from enemy action. Aerial attack was expected, so walls of sandbags were built in front of important public buildings to absorb the blast of bombs. The gang here is doing a grand job. It is ironic that Preston Town Hall, having been so carefully preserved throughout the war, would burn down shortly afterwards. This part of the building housed the Food Office, which issued ration books, so was absolutely vital. Clearly it was not possible to sandbag the whole town, but there were other steps that could be taken. Shops taped their windows in a criss-cross pattern so that if the window was shattered during aerial attack, there would be less danger of passers-by

Top: Cotton spinning and weaving were cottage industries in Preston before the industrial revolution. When mechanised processes were first invented, the workers opposed them fiercely, fearing that these new-fangled machines would take away their livelihoods. Their antagonism was sufficient to discourage Preston-born inventor and entrepreneur Richard Arkwright from setting up a factory there. However, in 1777 the town's first mechanised mill, called The Factory, was opened by Messrs Collison and Watson. The Horrocks business started in 1791, and in the Victorian era the industry really gained momentum, with more and more mills providing employment for more and more workers. Greenbank Mills started up in 1836, and that is where, more than a century later, these young ladies were photographed. They were no doubt aware, even as they learned their skills during the 1940s, that the heyday of the cotton industry was past - but they could not have known just how badly the industry would suffer over the next couple of decades. Not only did post-war years bring a flood of cheap foreign imports, but the new synthetic materials became fashionable, and the demand for British-made cotton goods dwindled rapidly. For many years the government did nothing to help, and finally in the late 1950s it took the drastic step of making substantial compensation available to mill-owners to scrap their plant so that labour and capital could be directed to more profitable enterprises - electronics, vehicles and aircraft, thus forcing more and more mills out of business.

being injured by flying glass. Also in the interests of public safety, white stripes were painted round street furniture as seen on this photograph. This was to help people who had to travel in blackout conditions; by picking out strategic kerbs, lamp-posts and other obstacles, there was less chance of people crashing into them. Sadly, many accidents did occur during blackouts, adding to the toll of wartime injuries and fatalities.

Do you remember when petrol stations looked like this? When petrol was measured in gallons, and you could fill your tank up and get change from a fiver? Dream on; but Withy Trees Service Station really does look rather attractive in this picture, and its five pumps on the forecourt, with those lovely illuminated shell-shaped heads, would become highly collectable items in years to come. However, once we had come to accept self-service shops and supermarkets, the introduction of self-service petrol stations was a logical next step. In the 1970s, garages began putting up big neon-lit canopies, installing automatic car washes, and selling sweets, pop, clothes and novelty goods along with car accessories; suddenly going along with Dad on Sunday morning to fill up the car became fun. The new, streamlined petrol pumps which appeared on the forecourts filled your tank up faster, but they weren't nearly as pretty ... Much earlier, Withy Trees used to be the terminus for the tram route up Garstang Road. The route was later extended because there were concerns that this junction was a dangerous place for the trams to stop. The name 'Withy Trees' is believed to have been given to the inn during the second half of the 19th century, in reference to the many willow trees which used to exist in this area.

Building a reputation

Whilst the art of working with wood may not be quite the oldest profession it certainly ranks amongst the most ancient. The Master Joiners and Builders of Preston who met together for the first time on March 18th 1850 would have been all too aware that their profession could quote scripture in support of their claims for special status amongst the craftsmen of the town.

The Walker family has been involved in the building industry in Preston ever since then when John and James Walker were instrumental in forming the Master Joiners and Builders of Preston Association.

But why were the joiners and builders getting together? The answer was 'to remove or ameliorate certain evils which for a length of time have been known to exist and which all parties connected with the trade have reason to deplore'. What the craftsmen were banding together to fight was joiners and builders competing against one another, contracting for work at prices lower than was thought possible. Those who joined the Association agreed to strictly adhere to its scale of prices.

And what a wonderful price list it was, with architraves priced at three farthings a foot and corn bins made from one inch oak at one shilling and tuppence the foot including lids, hinges and nails. Animal troughs at one and threepence a foot reminds us of a by-gone age as does wainscoting - wooden wall panelling - at sixpence a square foot, or three shillings in oak. Doors, roofs and ceilings come as no surprise but how many of us today would think of getting a joiner to make us a toilet? Back then a three foot wide water closet with backs and elbows in mahogany with a front seat cover would set one back four pounds and ten shillings, even

Below: *A Walker family portrait with founder, Roger Walker, on the back row, far right.*

before the plumber came along to do his work - a luxury item indeed.

Today's R Walker & Sons (Preston) Ltd was founded by Roger Walker; in 1896 he established himself in business in Back Lane (now Market Street) opposite Trinity Church working as a carpenter, joiner and funeral director and trading from three cottages with a workshop on the first floor.

For the times Roger Walker was quite unique in having obtained his City & Guilds Certificates not only in Carpentry & Joinery in 1886 but also went on to obtain a similar qualification in Brickwork & Masonry two years later. That dual qualification was a clear indicator of his powers of application and persistence.

In the early part of the 20th century what had in the course of years become R Walker & Sons was involved in building many of the buildings which shaped Preston town centre as we now know it, including working on Miller Arcade.

Roger Walker had three sons: Jack, Norbert and Herbert who all helped in running the business until the start of the second world war in 1939. The war affected the business not least by splitting the family. Norbert was called up to serve in the forces, Jack carried on running the business whilst Herbert, along with many of the firm's joiners, was directed to work at Dick, Kerrs (English Electric) as a pattern maker for aircraft manufacturing. Later, in conjunction with the War Office, the firm converted the Dunkenhalgh Hotel at Rishton into a military HQ and would be involved in other War Office contracts including the manufacture of thousands of munitions boxes in conjunction with Page & Taylor's timber merchants of Watery Lane.

Even after the end of World War II life was not easy. The construction industry was still depressed, raw materials were rationed and licences had to be obtained in order to buy timber. Fuel coupons were introduced which, along with labour shortages, made the immediate post-war years difficult.

Jack Walker who had continued to run the business throughout the war was joined by his son Kenneth in 1946.

Top: *Walker's original Back Lane workshop.* ***Above:*** *Roger Walker's City And Guilds certificate from 1888.*

Norbert Walker continued his career as a Clerk of Works for the War Office after 1945 and never returned to the company. Herbert Walker however did return, working as a joiner whilst also pursuing a career as a respected tutor in Building Construction at Preston Technical College.

Herbert's eldest son David Walker joined the company as an apprentice joiner in 1953. After seven years apprenticeship he left the company for two years to carry out his National Service before returning to take up a more managerial role.

Whilst traditionally the company had always undertaken small domestic works David and Ken now endeavoured to obtain more commercial work, particularly local authority contracts and maintenance works on all government buildings around the Preston area. That strategy was successful and due to the continuing growth of the company the first floor of the Market Street premises was demolished and larger workshop facilities were built at the rear of the building incorporating redundant alleyways and backyards.

R Walker & Sons (Preston) Ltd has always held an active role in the promotion of the building industry in the local area. Indeed it can boast four past presidents of the Preston & District Building Trades Employers Association, more than any other current member.

The late 1980s proved pivotal for the company when in 1988 with the

purchase of adjacent property for the manufacture of uPVC windows and doors. The Walker Windows name has since become synonymous with both quality and integrity within the domestic and commercial replacement uPVC window markets.

The two cousins, David and Kenneth Walker, were to enjoy a working relationship which would last more than a quarter of a century. Sadly however Ken died prematurely in 1980. David was joined in the running of the company by Graham his eldest son who had served a three year apprenticeship. Grant, David's youngest son, joined the business in 1987 whilst studying for a degree in Building Surveying.

David, Graham and Grant have increased the growth of the company each year through quality workmanship and the firm's reputation as one of Preston's oldest family companies. An enviable client portfolio has been established which includes Lancashire County Council, Preston NHS Trust and Blackpool, Wyre and Fylde NHS Trust.

And though Preston prices may be somewhat higher now than in 1850 the company still guarantees to present a highly competitive quote.

Above left: David Walker (centre) with sons Graham (left) and Grant (right). ***Below:*** The Walker Windows Premises on Market Street, West.

Historic Lessons

'Education, education, education' was a long remembered electoral war cry of Prime Minister Tony Blair. Yet although the words of politicians are seldom recalled for very long the memories we have of our schooldays linger with us all our lives.

But even the measure of an entire lifetime is nothing compared to the longevity of some of our educational establishments.

Centuries of Christian tradition underpin the education provided by Kirkham Grammar School which was founded as a charity school in 1549 and which consequently celebrated its 450th anniversary in 1999.

Indeed the school's roots can be traced back even further than the reign of Henry VIII's short-lived son Edward VI, to the chantry school attached to St Michael's Church, Kirkham, as long ago as the 13th century. It was there in the church grounds that the school remained until it moved to occupy its present site on Ribby Road in 1911.

Back in 1585 however, during the reign of Queen Elizabeth the first, the Thirty Men of Kirkham, a group which administered parish business, took over responsibility for the school. It appears they did not always perform their duties particularly well for by the early part of the 17th century the school had fallen into disrepair and had been without a master for seven years.

Remarkably Isabell Birly, a humble alehouse keeper, came to the rescue in 1621 when she presented the Thirty Men of Kirkham with £30 in her apron for the school's restoration.

Although £30 was a substantial amount of money in the 17th century, it was not enough to keep a school running. In 1655 however Henry

Above: The school tapestry showing Isabell Birly in her apron and presenting the Thirty Men of Kirkham with £30 for the restoration of the school. Below: A view of the school, 1995.

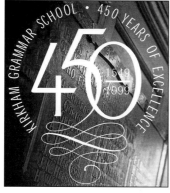

Colburn, an old boy of the school, left land and a large sum of money to the school in his will, putting it in the trust of the Company of Drapers in London. Then

began a long and cherished partnership between the company and the school which has continued to the present day, though the Drapers surrendered control of the school in 1944 after having endowed it with large and impressive extensions in 1938. The connection with the Drapers is recalled in the School Crest; on the shield are the doves of Kirkham township together with the triple coronets of the Drapers' Company.

Independent status ceased temporarily in 1944 when the school became a voluntary aided boys' grammar school. A further major building extension, the Norwood Science Building was opened in 1965, and itself subsequently extended later. In 1979 the Board of Governors took the bold decision to revert to independent status and Kirkham Grammar School admitted girls to became a co-educational school for the first time in its history.

In 1991 the school established its own preparatory department

in a new purpose built school on land it owned adjacent to the senior school. A superb floodlit sport turf pitch capable of accommodating hockey in winter and twelve tennis courts in summer was added in the same year. Meanwhile a flourishing partnership with BAE Systems was established which led to the opening of a state of the art Technology Centre designated as an International Centre of Excellence. Other developments included a new sixth form centre, languages centre, a library, 11 acres of new playing fields and a spacious new dining complex.

The last decade of the 20th century witnessed a remarkable growth in the school's popularity and standing too, demonstrated by a rise in pupil numbers from 500 to 900.

Following two successful full inspections the headmaster Mr Barrie Stacey was admitted to membership of the prestigious Headmasters and Headmistresses' Conference in June 2000 confirming Kirkham Grammar School's status as one of the country's leading independent schools. Appropriately the same year witnessed the school's best ever GCSE Advanced Level examination results and a record Oxbridge entry. In addition to its academic successes Kirkham Grammar School has also emerged as one of the country's top sporting schools. The school is also renowned for the quality of its music, art, science and drama.

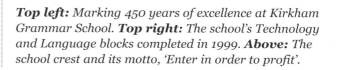

Little wonder that numbers continue to grow and competition for places at one of Lancashire's oldest educational institutions is stronger than ever. Today Kirkham Grammar School is looking forward with confidence to celebrating its 500th anniversary in the year 2049!

Top left: Marking 450 years of excellence at Kirkham Grammar School. Top right: The school's Technology and Language blocks completed in 1999. Above: The school crest and its motto, 'Enter in order to profit'.

Planting an education

With its own golf course and veterinary operating theatre Myerscough College is certainly a college with a difference.

Lancashire County Council formally established what would evolve into the Myerscough College in 1894 when it took the tenancy of Home Farm at Hutton, three miles south-west of Preston. The 147 acre farm was initially rented from Squire Rawstorne of Hutton for £2 18 shillings per acre; five years later the County Council bought the 289 acre farm from him for £29,000.

The Technical Instruction Committee of Lancashire County Council had used income from a local 'whisky tax' collected by the Customs & Excise service to establish the new 'Farm Institute' as the college was then known.

Prior to 1894, agricultural classes had been held at the Harris Institute in Preston, which was the forerunner of the University of Central Lancashire. In 1892 there were seven agriculture students attending classes at the Harris where the syllabus then comprised General Principles of Agriculture, Agricultural Chemistry, Mechanics and Steam, Agricultural Book-keeping and Veterinary Surgery.

At that time, in addition to the classes in Preston, practical classes in Cheese and Butter-making were financed by the County Council and were held at suitable local farms throughout the County Palatine of Lancashire, from Ulverston in the north to Halewood in the south and as far as Bacup to the east. Those classes were well attended, mainly by farming families keen to learn the intricacies of modern dairy product manufacture.

Above: Machine milking at Hutton in the 1940s.
Left: A lecture at Winmarleigh Hall, circa 1950.
Below: Hutton College pictured in the late 1950s.

In 1912 a new processing dairy, hostel and classrooms were built at Hutton and in the same year classes in Horticulture commenced. In 1917 instruction in poultry-keeping began to be provided for soldiers who would be discharged from the armed forces during and following World War I. Further expansion in student numbers took place during the 1920s and 30s eventually accommodating up to 80 resident students; despite increasing numbers Hutton would however remain the institute's only site until after the second world war.

In 1947 a second site at Winmarleigh Hall near Garstang, 20 miles north of Hutton, was purchased - £16,000 was paid for 42 acres. This was augmented by a further 291 acres, bought for £23,000 the following year. The agriculture courses moved to Winmarleigh, and forty male students were accommodated at this attractive but somewhat isolated manor house and estate. The dairying, horticulture and poultry courses remained at Hutton. At the same time part-time classes in agricultural subjects began to be developed throughout Lancashire and in 1959 the Extra Mural department was formally established. That work expanded rapidly and by 1966 there were 700 part-time students attending classes being arranged and taught by the college throughout the North West.

Despite such diversification, or perhaps because of it, in the early 1960s it was decided that a single centre accommodating all the College's services to further education, higher education and part-time students should be established. And so in 1969 Her Majesty The Queen opened the newly built Myerscough College in Bilsborrow. Thirty years later, in 1999, Her Majesty and The Duke of Edinburgh would again visited Myerscough this time to open the £3 million Fitzherbert-Brockholes Learning Resource Centre.

The College has continued to grow and to diversify over the years, with the commercial market coming to have increasing importance. Commercial sectors have been developed on the campus, providing excellent resources for students as well as offering a public service. Those commercial areas now comprise: the Plant Centre and Plant World, Stumble Inn, a Golf Academy, Sports Centre and Conference Centre (The Bowland Suite).

But why do people choose to come to Myerscough? The college is one of the very few land-based colleges in the UK, and it is one of the largest. Not only does the college provide Further Education, Higher Education and part-time courses but it also offers several unique facilities such as its Golf Academy, Animal Academy and Equine Centre as well as offering excellent accommodation for students aged 16 and above.

Despite its illustrious past the college is keen to plan for the future, not merely continuing to offer a quality education but to also expand its facilities; today new teaching blocks, a new equine centre and more accommodation are already on the drawing board.

Top left: The Horticultural Department at Myerscough College, 1986. ***Above left:*** *Veterinary Nursing.* ***Below:*** *Myerscough College, 2001.*

Building on experience

Perhaps one thing which helps us define the closing decades of the 20th century was the appearance of hundreds, indeed thousands, of prefabricated steel clad buildings. When did the first one appear, do you remember it? Who can say, but such buildings have slowly and inexorably changed the urban landscape in the way that Accrington brick did in the 19th century. No matter where one goes in Lancashire, or anywhere else in Britain, one is seldom out of sight of at least one of these buildings which astonishingly seem to be able to spring up in just days.

Preston's J Wareing & Son (Wrea Green) Ltd, based unsurprisingly at Wrea Green, is today well known all over Lancashire as a firm specialising in the erection of steel framed buildings. In fact the firm's reputation extends much further than the north-west and the company has supplied buildings to places as far afield as the Falkland

Islands and the Sudan as well as the many islands off mainland Britain.

Nor has the firm restricted itself to supplying simple corru-

gated metal sheds and warehouses: at Wareings the firm's main asset is its adaptability, being able to produce whatever the customer needs as economically as possible. Such flexibility has resulted in the firm obtaining contracts for buildings ranging from the shopping area at Ribby Hall Leisure Village, the Mazda car showroom in Southport and the 200 tons of steelwork fabricated to build the new mosque and cultural centre at Wimberley Street in Blackburn, a building constructed in two phases spread over a three year period.

Whether it is sports halls or potato stores which are asked for Wareings has built them all, and it has been doing so for a very long time indeed.

The business was founded in 1909 by wheelwrights and joiners George and James Wareing.

Working as wheelwrights and joiners the Wareings provided a huge range of services to farmers in and around Wrea Green; not just cart wheels for the horse drawn vehicles then still used in their thousands but the hundreds of different items which were, still within living memory, normally crafted from wood: feeding troughs, barn doors, feed barriers, fences and hen huts.

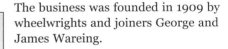

Top: *The late Harry Wareing (centre) with sons Peter (left) and Andrew (right).*
Above left and left: *Typical examples of early agricultural buildings.*

kits could be provided complete with instructions enabling customers to erect their own buildings using their own or local labour. The company would eventually be producing up to fifteen such prefabricated buildings each week, two thirds of which would be provided in kit form.

Sadly Harry Wareing passed away in 2000. Today the firm is run by his two sons Peter and Andrew helped by a staff of over 50 including five of Harry's grandchildren: Robin, Sally, Neil, Christopher and Richard. The large staff of fully trained people enables the company to fabricate steelwork to produce a variety of building types whilst an in-house joinery department, an echo of the firm's early origins, still manufactures many products from wood including doors and window frames.

Top left: An early Wareing sheep building.
Left: A Wareing steel frame unit erected for S & M Chemicals. Below: A partially erected unit clearly showing the main portal framework and cladding support system. Bottom: The Equestrian Centre at Ribby Hall featuring timber space boarding as cladding combined with facing stonework to the vertical faces.

But as farming methods changed over the years so did the firm's products, not least with an increasing concentration on prefabricated farm buildings. Of course the material of choice was still wood and Wareings' timber cow kennels for example would become a familiar sight on farms up to a hundred miles from Preston.

A big selling point of such buildings was that they could be made and delivered in kit form for erection on site. That experience would pay major dividends for the business in the long run. By the early 1970s it was evident that a sea change was in progress. The firm's catalogue still featured wooden cow kennels but new materials, corrugated roofing, steel pillars and asbestos sheeting were clearly pushing the older material out.

By the 1980s warehouses and industrial units on industrial estates were often being described as 'barn like'. It was an accurate reflection of their origins. Building prefabricated dairy units, storage buildings and cow kennels for agricultural clients provided the skills and expertise for Wareings to begin to offer its services to the industrial sector. As pioneers of 'kit' building the firm was now able to offer new customers a specialised service. Fabricated to individual requirements with a choice of many types of cladding

Planning Preston

E quipped with little more than a drawing board propped up on two bricks, a T-square and lots of hope Gerald Cassidy left his job with Lancashire County Council in 1957 and started his own business as an architect and planner working from his home in Penwortham. A former pupil of St Augustine's School and Preston Catholic College, and with his roots in Frenchwood, Gerald would prove to be a true Prestonian, always retaining a keen love for the town, especially Preston North End FC.

Gerald's very first project was to work on an extension for the Preston Ice Cold Storage Company, and more commissions soon followed. The new venture flourished and in 1959 Gerald was able to move his office from his home to Chapel Street taking on David Bennett and Fred Shorrock as trainees; a year later Gerald took Bernard Ashton as a partner. The two partners had much in common, each having seen National Service in the Royal Engineers prior to working in the County Architect's Department.

David Bennett whose dynamism would be a major factor in the firm's growth over the years became a partner in 1970; by the millennium he would eventually have become senior partner presiding over more than 60 partners and staff with branches in Greater Manchester, Halton, Merseyside and Windermere. In common with the firm's founders David could also boast of having deep roots in Preston having been born in Fulwood and attending Preston Grammar school as did Peter Whiteside who became a partner in 1979 remaining so until retirement to a consultancy in 2001. Other partners are Nick Hayes, Dave Cockrell, Mike Hartley, Alistair Baines and Phil Gornall. Fred Shorrock who was taken on in 1959 would still be with the firm more than forty years later, employed as a Technical Associate; he would come to typify the long standing relationship that exists between the firm and its members of staff. The current partners are proud to continue the family atmosphere that was part of Gerald Cassidy's original practice philosophy.

Over the decades however much else has changed. The T-square and drawing board on two bricks have long been sup-

Above: *A 25th Anniversary picture of founder Gerald Cassidy (second left) with Bernard Ashton, second Partner (far right), Peter Whiteside, Partner (far left), and David Bennett, Partner (second right).* **Left and below:** *Award winning projects by the firm, the Nat West Bank and Winckley Court office development.*

planted by the latest computerised technology, both in the CAD (Computer Aided Design) units used by the technical staff and the software programs which serve the Administration.

The Cassidy & Ashton partnership, known to the trade as C + A, are not only architects. In recent years they have established a flourishing Building Surveyors Division in Preston, Bury and Halton, all under the direction of Chartered Surveyor Phil Gornall. CA-Environment, specialising in Building Services Engineering and C + A Planning Consultancy are more recent additions to the comprehensive consultancy services now offered by the Cassidy + Ashton Group.

Over the years Cassidy + Ashton have been involved in many Preston projects being involved in both preserving the past and contributing to the future. The restoration of Miller Arcade to its former glory is a prime example of C + A's conservation work. Other award winning projects include offices in Winckley Square, Winckley Court; new premises for the Lancashire Evening Post; Nat West Bank Fishergate; the Waterfront Pub and Marina, Preston Dock; the South Ribble Council Offices and the former Sainsbury's premises on Ringway. Churches and schools have figured prominently too with churches in Penwortham, Fulwood, Lancaster University, Morecambe, Blackburn and schools in Fulwood, Penwortham, Ingol, Avenham, Bamber Bridge and Stonyhurst College.

As Cassidy + Ashton has expanded so has the diversity of the partnership's commissions. By the opening years of the 21st century projects in progress would include shopping centres, pubs, restaurants, schools, offices, church restorations, golf clubs, hospitals, residential nursing homes and cinemas.

Gerald Cassidy and Bernard Ashton, the original C + A, have now retired from the practice, though Gerald still retains a keen interest as a consultant and is delighted at the fulfilment of his 'lots of hope'.

Today's partners, working from their East Cliff offices, still aim to ensure that despite the firm having grown to be one of the major practices in the North West, their personal relationships with clients remain exactly as they were in the days of a 'drawing board on two bricks'.

This page: *Other award winning projects by Cassidy + Ashton, The Waterfront Pub and Marina, Preston Docks (top left), Preston Royal Infirmary, now a housing project (top right), restoration of Miller Arcade (centre) and the former Sainsbury's site on Ringway (below).*

Painting the town gold

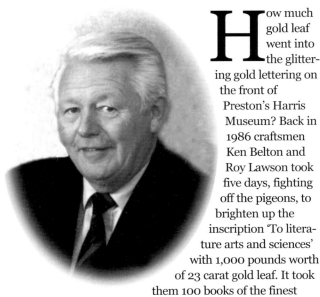

How much gold leaf went into the glittering gold lettering on the front of Preston's Harris Museum? Back in 1986 craftsmen Ken Belton and Roy Lawson took five days, fighting off the pigeons, to brighten up the inscription 'To literature arts and sciences' with 1,000 pounds worth of 23 carat gold leaf. It took them 100 books of the finest quality double gold leafing to complete the work which would be visible miles away for decades.

Ken and Roy were working for Bernard Watson, one of the north-west's leading signwriting, painting and decorating companies, a local firm which has a history that goes back to the last quarter of the 19th century.

Established as John Corbishley & Sons Ltd in 1878 the company passed into the hands of the present management in 1979, and now trades as Bernard Watson (inc J Corbishley & Sons Ltd). Since then it has continued to build on its already enviable reputation for the quality of its craftsmanship, the professionalism of its operatives and the excellence of its customer service. In January 2001 the company went one step

ahead of its competitors by achieving the prestigious Investors in People Award. But where did it all begin?

The founder of the business was John Corbishley; his original premises were in North Road where the firm would remain for 48 years. It was not until 1926 that the company would move - though it didn't go far, just across the road, in fact, to what are still its premises at 170 North Road.

John Corbishley's business was soon to turn into a family affair with six of his children following in his footsteps and becoming directors of the business. His grandchildren also joined the company completing apprenticeships in either painting and decorating or plumbing.

In time ownership of the company passed from John Corbishley to his eldest son William who, in his turn, would pass the business on to his son, also called William.

On 1st November 1979 the company was bought by Bernard Watson. At that time John Corbishley & Sons employed eight tradesmen, the same number as Bernard Watson, making a total of 16 time served craftsmen following the amalgamation.

Top left: Owner Bernard Watson.
Above: A Corbishley family picture with founder John Corbishley (front row, second right).
Left: Pictured, William Corbishley (second row, fourth from the left) son of John, William's son also named William (fourth row, fourth from the left) and George Corbishley (front row, first left) father of Beth Cribbin who still works at the company.

One employee, Beth Cribbin, is the great-granddaughter of John Corbishley; she had begun working for the company in 1975 under William Corbishley the younger; and would continue working for Bernard Watson after the take-over.

Astonishingly more than 20 years after the acquisition of the Corbishley business Bernard Watson was still employing half the original work force of J Corbishley & Sons, the remainder having left only due to retirement.

John Corbishley & Sons Ltd had been renowned for its ecclesiastical work around Preston, a reputation which was to be carried forward by Bernard Watson. Examples of such fine artwork undertaken in recent years can be seen at St Wilfrid's Longridge, St Mary's, Chipping and St Mary's and St James Church, Scorton where wonderful fine artwork was uncovered and restored. In January 2001 the company was given the task of refurbishing St Mary and All Saints' church, Whalley, going back in time to the traditional method of lime washing.

Other prestigious work has been carried out on St George's Hall in Blackburn and Stonyhurst College, which has had connections with the business since 1925.

Despite providing a service to all kinds of clients it is perhaps the work the firm has carried out on historic buildings which has made its reputation. When it came to the redecoration of Preston's historic Samlesbury Hall the owners entrusted the work to Bernard Watson in the full knowledge that the building's delicate period fabric was in expert hands. Similarly the major refurbishment of St Peter's Cathedral, Lancaster, involving plain and highly detailed decorative paintwork requiring the extensive use of stenciling would result in an acclaimed transformation of the interior. The work was not only acknowledged as a superb example of skilled craftsmanship but also contributed to the project receiving a RIBA award for excellence.

Bernard Watson established his company in 1967. He had served his time with a high class painting contractor in Preston.

But not content with simply serving his time Bernard went on after his apprenticeships to gain an impressive range of further technical qualifications. In 1976 Ken Belton who also had an impressive range of technical qualifications joined him.

Today the company is run by managing director, Bernard Watson, along with directors Ken Belton and Bernard's youngest daughter Clare Watson, with over 35 years of 'hands on' experience of contracts both large and small, the company can demonstrate a proven track record in a wide range of environments, from industrial and commercial jobs to specialist ecclesiastical projects, leisure and domestic contracts.

Top left: The completed transformation of St Mary's, Euxton. Top right: Samlesbury Hall's delicate period fabric, expertly redecorated by Bernard Watson. Above: Staff pictured taking part in the Preston Guild, 1992. Below: Bernard Watson and staff outside the company premises on North Road.

Turning pigs into planks

The story of Thompson Builders Merchants began in the 1950s whilst the firm's founder Thomas Wilfrid Thompson was still living on his father's farm.

After completing his apprenticeship at Beathams, a prominent joinery firm in Preston, and having gained further experience with building and civil engineering contractors in the area Thomas decided it was time to set out in business on his own.

And so, with no more than a bag of tools, an old van, a 24ft by 12ft cabin, which then housed an old saw, and the sheer determination to succeed Thomas Thompson took the first steps that would eventually lead to today's Thompson Builders Merchants now based at Waverley Park Mill in Miller Road, Ribbleton.

At first the majority of joinery work was of an agricultural nature and, as such, conventional working hours did not exist. Thomas never turned a job down however - and he was never one to waste money once he had worked long and hard to get it; he saved and he saved.

By 1963 Thomas Thompson had saved enough money to make a down-payment on the then run-down Hill Top Farm in Barton. From the farm he started farming pigs whilst continuing to do his joinery work.

Some years after buying Hill Top Farm Thomas began selling plywood to local farmers, followed shortly afterwards by corrugated roofing materials and other products used mainly in the livestock and agricultural industry.

The roofing materials and joinery side of the business grew steadily through the 1970s by which time Andrew Pemberton had joined the workforce from school as an apprentice joiner. Today Andrew now does the majority of timber buying and selling for the company.

By the beginning of the 1980s the merchanting side of the business had become dominant and it was clear that for growth to continue more premises would have to be acquired. With money mainly generated from the Thompson pig breeding company and a loan from the bank Thomas was able to buy a yard at Stocks Road, Ashton.

To run the yard Thomas took on Miles Stapleton whom he had known since boyhood; Miles had in fact also been the first 'rep' to call at Hill Top Farm in his capacity as timber salesman for Horsley Smith, from where he had later become the manager at Jewsons St Anne's branch.

Within the first year of the opening of the Stocks Road yard it became clear that the company needed a sales person and so Miles Stapleton brought in Peter Ely who had been a representative with Miles' previous employer.

By the mid 1980s the business was still growing and Andrew Pemberton, Miles Stapleton and Peter Ely had all become directors of the company. It was during this time that Georgina, the founder's daughter came to help with the administrative side of the business; she

Above: Founder Thomas Wilfrid Thompson pictured at Hill Top Farm in 1967 with daughter Georgina.

THOMPSON BUILDERS MERCHANTS (PRESTON) LTD.

TIMBER AND BUILDERS MERCHANTS

110 STOCKS ROAD, ASHTON
PRESTON, PR2 2TB

TEL: 01772 728826
FAX: 01772 723391

WAVERLEY PARK, MILLER ROAD
RIBBLETON, PRESTON, PR1 5QS

TEL: 01772 704848
FAX: 01772 651260

became credit controller and would subsequently became a director herself.

Due to pressure from the local planning authority Thompsons were however soon faced with having to find additional premises so that they could continue in business. In 1988 the company was able to acquire new premises at Miller Road, Ribbleton which covered around three and a quarter acres of land and had more than 50,000 square feet of shop and storage space - and was conveniently located just a little over a mile from junction 31 on the motorway.

It is from these premises, as well as the one at Stocks Road, Ashton, that Thompsons continue to trade today.

Despite its long history the company inevitably moves on; Miles Stapleton retired in 1999 and Mark Lee who had been with the company since he was 17 and ran the Stocks Road branch was made a director.

Sadly the firm's founder, Thomas Wilfrid Thompson, died in May 2000; he left his company to his daughter Georgina. Thomas also expressed the hope that his son-in-law Graham would join the firm and support Georgina in running the business. That wish would be fulfilled, Georgina and Graham now both work in the firm.

Georgina Dewhurst dedicates this story to her mother and late father with gratitude.

Above: *A Thompson Builders Merchants letterhead.*
Below: *The present board, (back row from left to right) Andrew Pemberton, Mark Lee and Peter Ely with (front row) Georgina and Harli (left) and Graham and Freddi.*

Women from the Auxiliary Territorial Service march to celebrate VE Day on 13th May 1945.

Acknowledgments

The publishers would like to thank
Ann Dennison at the Harris Library, Brian Parkin, Ann Murray and
David Hunt for his help in the course proof-reading.

Thanks are also due to
Margaret Wakefield who penned the editorial text
and Steve Ainsworth for his copywriting skills